PEWDIEPIE

PEWDIEPIE

THE ULTIMATE UNOFFICIAL FAN GUIDE TO THE WORLD'S BIGGEST YOUTUBER

Jo Berry

This edition first published in Great Britain in 2015 by
Orion
an imprint of the Orion Publishing Group Ltd
Carmelite House
50 Victoria Embankment
London EC4Y 0DZ
An Hachette UK Company

1 3 5 7 9 10 8 6 4 2

Picture credits :
Fotolia: page 6 (bottom), 8, 19 (top left), 22, 28. 34. 36 (left), 37 (top left,
bottom right), 39 (bottom), 44, 45, 50, 51 (middle right); Getty Images: page 9
(top right), 12, 15 (top), 25, 26, 29, 31,33, 42, 43, 47, 51 (top), 53, 55, 61; IBL/REX:
poster, page 6 (top left), 7, 19 (top right), 41, 45, 63; PA Images: page 18, 21, 48;
Picture Perfect/REX: page 2, 11 (top right), 23, 35, 37, 51 (bottom).
All other illustrations: iStock by Getty Images

A CIP catalogue record for this book is available
from the British Library.

ISBN: 978 1 4091 6206 3

Printed in Italy

The Orion Publishing Group's policy is to use papers that are natural,
renewable and recyclable and made from wood grown in sustainable forests.
The logging and manufacturing processes are expected to conform to the
environmental regulations of the country of origin.

Every effort has been made to fulfil requirements with regard to reproducing
copyright material. The author and publisher will be glad to rectify any
omissions at the earliest opportunity.

www.orionbooks.co.uk

CONTENTS

PEWDIEPIE

> 'AiN'T
> NO PARTY
> liKE A
> PEWDIEPIE
> PARTY!'

He's the most popular person on YouTube, with over 34 million subscribers at the start of 2015 and a jaw-dropping eight billion video views. PewDiePie – also known as Felix Kjellberg, or just Pewds – is a real internet phenomenon, whose popularity grows every day. Funny, goofy and rude, his energetic videos of him playing video games and his weekly vlogs are must-see entertainment, and are all the more fun because he screams so much when he gets to a scary part in a game!

When he's not playing games or pranks online, PewDiePie devotes time and his own money to charity – when he reached 10 million subscribers, he encouraged fans to donate to Charity: Water and donated a dollar of his own money for every 500 views of his video about the campaign, raising over $400,000, and he helped raise over $630,000 for Save The Children in 2014, too.

Funny, mad, silly, hilarious to watch and surprisingly shy, it looks like YouTube's most popular guy is set for world domination!

THE EARLY DAYS

Felix Kjellberg was born in Gothenburg in Sweden – the home town of Volvo cars, nineties' pop band Ace of Base, and now PewDiePie!

When he was little, Felix (which means 'happy' in Latin!) started drawing a lot at school and teachers told his parents he could be an artist – but he just wanted to draw video game characters like Yoshi, Sonic the Hedgehog, Donkey Kong and Mario. Playing video games was his favourite thing to do, but he didn't have a console at home because his parents knew he'd be on it too much. When he wasn't well, his mum would rent a Super Nintendo for him to play on – not surprisingly, Felix was ill quite a lot growing up!

In 2008, after leaving school, he went on to study a degree in the rather impressive-sounding subject Industrial Economics and Technology Management at Chalmers University of Technology in Gothenburg, and in his spare time he created art in Photoshop – some of which was exhibited and sold in a local gallery. He used the money to buy a new computer, and started making gaming videos on it, which he had always wanted to do. He enjoyed it so much that he left university after three years to focus on his YouTube career. Even Felix himself thinks this was slightly mad: 'It was utterly absurd. To get into Chalmers for Industrial Economics you need

straight As, but somehow I was happier selling hot dogs and making my own gaming videos,' he told Swedish radio.

Those gaming videos are what have made Pewds a star. Beginning in April 2010 when he was still in college, he started filming himself playing video games, including Minecraft (the first video he made) and horror games like Amnesia: The Dark Descent. Viewers can watch the action as Felix walks through the games, and his reactions are filmed and appear in a box at the corner of the screen. It's those reactions that made him famous – Felix screams when he's scared, jumps when there's a shock, and swears just like everyone else when he gets stuck in the middle of a game.

Felix named his online persona PewDiePie – the Pew being the noise that laser guns in games make, and Die because dying happened in a lot of the horror games he was playing. Originally, PewDie was the name of his YouTube account but when he forgot his password – duh! – Felix renamed himself PewDiePie, with the Pie being partly thanks to a noise he makes, and partly a homage to pies!

For the first year of PewDiePie being online, Felix only posted game walkthroughs, but in September 2011 he began posting weekly vlogs, answering fans' questions, googling himself, opening his mail on camera, and taking his video camera out with him when he visited places like New York and London. He also included his girlfriend, Marzia, whom he met online, in some of his videos, too, and even got her to play some of the scarier horror games like Amnesia with him online!

When they met, Felix wasn't making any money from his YouTube channel, and worked odd jobs so he and Marzia could be together. However, since then his PewDiePie channel has grown and grown, and Marzia has her own really successful channel, too, called CutiePieMarzia.

PEWDIEPIE

STATS AND FACTS

Full name: Felix Arvid Ulf Kjellberg

Nickname: Pewdie, Pewds, PewDiePie

Date of birth: 24 October 1989

Hometown: Felix lives in Brighton now but he was born in Gothenburg in Sweden

Date he launched his YouTube channel: 29 April 2010

Favourite animals: Dogs — Felix has two pugs, Edgar and Maya

Best friend: Felix has three good friends from junior high school in Sweden, while his best YouTube friends are Cinnamon Toast Ken and Cryaotic

Most hated food: Pewds hates eggs!

Phobias: He actually finds horror games scary! But that's how he started playing games on YouTube — he decided to video himself playing frightening games so he didn't feel so alone

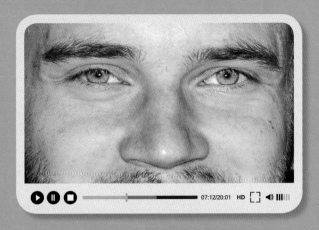

Secret talent: He's always loved drawing and has exhibited some of his artwork at his grandmother's gallery in Fiskebäckskil in Sweden. One painting of Little Red Riding Hood as seen from the wolf's mouth was sold and he used the money to buy his first computer

Star sign: Scorpio

Hair colour: Brown

First video: the first game PewDiePie videoed himself playing was Minecraft

Favourite movies: *A Clockwork Orange* and *Donnie Darko*

Favourite band: Radiohead

Fascinating fact: PewDiePie is so popular with the gaming community that he now makes cameo appearances in some of the games! He's appeared in Cry of Fear and Octodad

07:12/20:01 HD

A DAY IN THE LIFE

So what does PewDiePie do all day in his Brighton home – does he just play games? Of course not, he's got two dogs to look after, remember?! He does try to post a video every day for his fans, so it means that a lot of Pewds' time is spent in front of his computer, but he does get time to hang out in the Brighton sunshine once in a while (though he still finds it odd when people recognise him on the street and come over to say hello!).

Here's an average day for PewDiePie...

Pewds *says* he likes to wake up early so he can get as much done as possible during the day, but he's also said he's very lazy, isn't a morning person, and likes to sleep – so we don't believe him!

When he does get up, he edits the videos he recorded the day before, ready to post them online, or records a new video of himself playing a game. This can take up much of the day. He often spends around eight hours making videos In hls room, with the window shut, of course, so his screams don't scare the neighbours.

If he has time, Pewds then reads some of the comments he gets online. And hopefully he's finished his work in the evening so he can spend time with Marzia, hanging out or going to the cinema. And yes, he and Marzia love to go and watch horror movies!

PEWDIEPIE AWARDS!

You can't be the most-watched person on YouTube without winning a few awards...

Since Felix launched his channel in October 2010, he has been nominated at the Streamy Awards for Best Gaming Channel, Show or Series and he has won these great accolades:

Most Popular Social Show Award and Sweden Social Star Award

Starcount Social Star Awards 2013

Held in Marina Bay Sands in Singapore, the Starcount Awards honoured the most successful films, actors, web stars and people across the world's biggest social media networks. Jessica Alba and Jeremy Piven hosted the ceremony, and awards went to Justin Bieber (Best Solo Artist), One Direction (Best Music Group) and Felix for his YouTube channel PewDiePie.

#Gaming Award
Shorty Awards 2013

The 5th annual Shorty Awards, held in New York in April 2013, recognised the best of social media. Award finalists were

'WHEN i STARTED MY YOUTUBE CHANNEL, i NEVER IMAGINED THAT ONE DAY iT WOULD BE THE MOST SUBSCRIBED CHANNEL iN THE WORLD AND THAT i WOULD BE PART OF SUCH A GREAT COMMUNITY.'

voted for on Twitter and the winners included American TV presenter Jimmy Kimmel, Michelle Obama, Justin Bieber and *The Fault in Our Stars* author John Green. PewDiePie shared his award with fellow gamer RandonsPlays.

Web Star: Gaming
Teen Choice Awards 2014

The Teen Choice Awards is, of course, the fun US awards show where winners get to take home their own surfboard. *The Fault in Our Stars* won a handful of awards, the Kardashians won for Best Reality Show, and Felix's fellow Brighton YouTuber, Zoella, won Choice Web Star in the Fashion/Beauty category. PewDiePie then won Choice Web Star: Gaming.

Most Popular YouTube Channel

PewDiePie was officially declared the most subscribed to YouTube channel of all time in August 2013. On 15 August, Felix's channel surpassed Ian Hecox and Anthony Padilla's Smosh to claim the **Number One** spot and figures released show that PewDiePie gets one new subscriber every 1.6 seconds. Wow.

BEING A BRO IN

THE BRO ARMY

Pewds calls his fans 'Bros' and uses a Brofist (fist bump) at the end of his videos, and it's become so popular that his Brofist logo now features on a range of clothes. Felix greets his Bro Army at public events, walking the red carpet to say hello to them, and one of the reasons he has so many followers online is that he listens to what they want him to do, often playing games that bros have suggested he try — even when he doesn't really want to...

And PewDiePie's Bros are pretty amazing themselves, having raised hundreds of thousands of dollars for charity — first for Charity: Water when he reached 10 million subscribers and more recently for Save the Children, where Pewds and his bros raised a fantastic $630,000.

To be a true Bro, subscribe to PewDiePie's channels, read this book, then take The Ultimate PewDiePie Quiz on page 60. Brofist if you get all the answers correct!

TRY A PEWDIEPIE CHALLENGE!

While some of the challenges and pranks Felix has videoed aren't for the faint hearted (really, don't try drinking hot sauce – he couldn't manage it), some are pretty fun to try out with your friends. So why not play...

The 7-Second Challenge

Write down seven challenges for your friend, and they write down seven for you. You have got just 7 seconds to complete each challenge, and the winner is the one who completes the most challenges in time! Here are some suggestions of challenges...

In 7 seconds...

1) name five dog breeds

2) read a sentence from the nearest book to hand

3) do a ridiculous dance

4) do a somersault

5) lick your elbow

6) put on trousers, a jumper and socks over your clothes

7) say the alphabet... backwards

8) apply lipstick without a mirror

9) draw a self-portrait while blindfolded

10) name five superheroes who don't have 'man' in their name (e.g. Batman)

11) walk from one side of the room to the other while balancing a book on your head — if it falls you have to go back to the beginning

12) name five countries beginning with the letter 'S'

13) find all four aces in a shuffled pack of cards

19

PEWDS' STYLE

Want to look like Pewds? Here's how:

You'll need:

1. a patterned sweater (these are very popular in Scandinavia, just check out Detective Sarah Lund in the Danish TV drama *The Killing* if you don't believe us)
2. a T-shirt, preferably with a logo or design on the front
3. jeans
4. a onesie or pyjama pants for those days when you don't leave the house
5. ruffled hair and, if you want to be really authentic, a beard!
6. a hoodie

Fans love Pewds' sense of style so much that he has launched his own clothing range. You can buy pyjama pants, a hat, a hoodie and T-shirts with the Brofist logo on them, as well as T-shirts with a cartoon image of PewDiePie at shop.pewdiepie.com.

PEWDIEPIE FOR PRESIDENT!

Imagine if PewDiePie were President for a day. What do you think he would do?

1) Create a National Game Day where everyone gets the day off to play games!

2) Put a pug dog's face on the national flag

3) Make the Brofist the official way of greeting people, instead of a handshake

4) Ask everyone to take the money they'd spend in one month on games and donate it to charity instead

5) Make Marzia Mrs President!

6) Use the Presidential plane to fly his family from Sweden and Marzia's from Italy to his home in Brighton for a party

7) Make sure every sweet shop in the world had to stock his favourite Swedish snacks

8) Ban mean comments online forever

9) Decree that all PewDiePie fan art should be displayed in the Louvre art gallery

10) Make sleeping an Olympic sport

PEWDIEPIE TRUE OR FALSE?

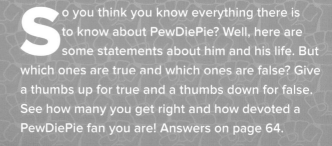

So you think you know everything there is to know about PewDiePie? Well, here are some statements about him and his life. But which ones are true and which ones are false? Give a thumbs up for true and a thumbs down for false. See how many you get right and how devoted a PewDiePie fan you are! Answers on page 64.

1) Felix met his girlfriend Marzia at a party for YouTubers.

2) He created his YouTube channel on 29 April 2010.

3) Felix named himself PewDiePie after he forgot his online password for his PewDie YouTube account.

4) He has lived in Sweden, Spain and England.

5) PewDiePie's girlfriend has her own YouTube channel, featuring videos of her singing.

6) The ending of the game The Last of Us was so shocking it is famous for rendering Felix completely speechless.

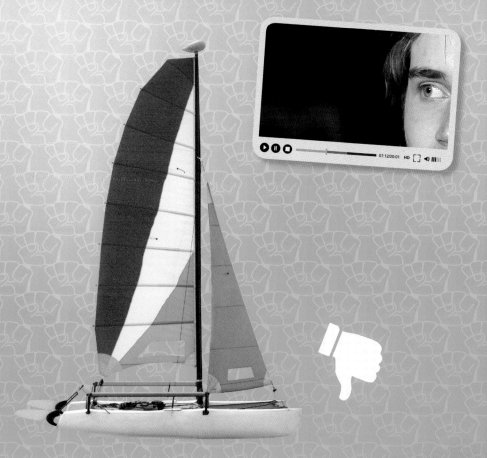

7) PewDiePie's YouTube channel has more subscribers than those of President Barack Obama, singer Beyoncé and pop band One Direction put together.
8) Felix has two pug dogs, named Edward and Maria.
9) He's appeared in a Hollywood movie playing himself, and his character is murdered.
10) He has to film himself in a room with the windows closed so his shouting doesn't disturb the neighbours.
11) PewDiePie records his videos months in advance of putting them on YouTube.
12) He's scared of thunder.
13) He says his girlfriend knows more about football and cars than he does!
14) He can play electric guitar.
15) He can sail a boat.

PLAY LIKE PEWDS!

F elix plays so many games he is an expert in many of them. While his horror game tactic seems to be 'scream and then run away' (which is often the best response for many of those games, or in real life if you happen upon a zombie), here are some tips for some of the more fun games he plays so you can raise your scores...

MINECRAFT

Many people are happy to wander their Minecraft worlds building structures and avoiding creepers. But if you do decide to take on the Ender Dragon, here are some tips to help you defeat it:

1. If you are fighting the Ender Dragon, you must make sure you're wearing armour.
2. Before you fight him, you need to take out the crystals at the top of the obsidian towers around him as the crystals heal him.
3. You need a bow and arrow to fight the Ender Dragon, as arrows are the only thing that hurts him.

BRIDGE CONSTRUCTOR

This free app kept Pewds amused for ages – although he was pretty rubbish at actually building the bridges, usually making something that broke in the middle meaning the people in cars going across plunged to their deaths! It's a great building game with over 30 levels of building bridges across valleys, canals or rivers using a variety of materials – the only limit is your budget. The level most people get stuck on is 7, where the bridge has to span a water-filled canyon, but here's a tip:

1. Build triangular-shaped supports that start narrow from concrete pillars below, and span wide to hold the maximum amount of stress on the bridge. And keep your fingers crossed when cars drive across!

SOCCER PHYSICS

PewDiePie says this addictive app is one of the easiest games ever, since you only have two players on each team and all you have to do is get the ball in your goal. However, the goal does get smaller. To win against another player just follow these rules (that you probably would get a yellow card for in a real match):

1. Use one of your players to push the other in the right direction.
2. Kicking an opponent repeatedly in the head causes them to lie down and be pretty useless.

OCTODAD

Pewds loves this game about a suit-wearing octopus disguised as a human. It's relatively simple to play, but here are some tips to make it more fun:

1. Tiptoe! If you raise your left tentacle slightly, then the right one straight after, and then alternate, you will tiptoe across the floor. It looks hilarious but is actually quite helpful when you want Octodad to be stealthy.
2. Silly biologists: When you get to the area where three biologists are standing in a hallway facing you, don't worry. All you have to do to get past them is grab the cover on the right-hand side so it is in front of you and then move towards them. Believe it or not, they'll completely ignore you.
3. Fancy some extra fun while playing? Send Octodad down the kids' slides in the aquarium, try getting him on the Segway (moving scooter) in the supermarket, and best of all, if you 'accidentally' put one of his tentacles on the grill when he is barbecuing burgers, he'll cook it... and squeal, too!

PEWDIEPIE'S GAMING TIPS

PewDiePie plays a lot of different types of games, but especially enjoys survival and horror ones. Many of the games he plays are online, so here are some bro tips for how to play safely while connecting with your friends:

Choose a safe game name

If you're going to be playing with people you don't know or who aren't close friends, make sure you use a name that doesn't reveal who you are. Don't have your name as part of it, and try to avoid using 'boy' or 'girl' in the name, too. After all, you'd never know PewDiePie's real name was Felix, would you? It's something you can have fun with, as you get to pick a cool name like SuperAwesomeDude100 or CatNinja. Though we've taken those two, so there.

Keep a secret

As well as having a safe game name, it's a good idea to be anonymous in other ways if you are playing online. If you're under 18, choose an avatar rather than using a webcam or a photo of yourself so strangers don't see what you look like. You can even get voice-altering features on some games so other gamers don't hear what you sound like either – and hey, it's fun playing a game when you sound like Darth Vader and it scares your fellow players, too.

Protect your personal information

You don't want to be hacked, so protect your information on any gaming accounts. Don't give out your name, address, phone number, user names or passwords, or your birthday to anyone online. And make sure you use strong, long passwords that only you and your parents know – and, no, PASSWORD1234 doesn't count!

Tell someone

Don't let another player get away with making you feel uncomfortable – tell a trusted adult. And remember, you can kick a player out of a game if they make you feel weird or are bullying you. Make sure you know how to block or report a player if you need to.

Think before you act

We're all bombarded with messages when reading or playing online. Don't act if someone asks for any personal information, or if they offer something that sounds too good to be true. Don't accept downloads from strangers, including cheat programs that may help you in games, as they may be carrying malware. And even think about what you share online with friends – remember, once it's online it is out of your control.

If things go wrong...

If you have accidentally shared too much online when signing up or playing a game, or you see something that upsets you, tell a trusted adult. You can also get them to check your privacy settings to make sure you are as safe online as you can possibly be.

HAPPY GAMING BROS!

PEWDS' FAVOURITE GAMES

PewDiePie loves video games, and he became popular for his game walkthroughs on YouTube because they were so full of enthusiasm. He started off with Minecraft and horror game videos, but more recently has played any game that takes his fancy! Of course, some of the games he plays – and the language he uses while playing them – are quite grown up and may only be suitable for older players.

All games are given **PEGI** ratings (kind of like movie certificates) to give an idea of how suitable they are. The ratings are:

3 – for all ages

7 – for most ages, may have frightening scenes

12 – mild bad language, some violence

16 – age 16 and over due to possible criminal scenes, violence, language, etc.

18 – adults only due to extreme scares or violence

You'll see the ratings for each of Felix's favourite games after the title.

www.pegi.info

Minecraft

Minecraft was one of the very first games Felix played for YouTube. It is, of course, the Mojang-created game where players get to build constructions out of cubes and play in various modes including creative, adventure and survival mode, where you have to gather resources and avoid falling into lava, starving to death and being attacked by various creatures. Launched in 2009, it was the most bought title on Xbox Live by 2012.

Amnesia: The Dark Descent

Want to hear PewDiePie scream? He does it often while playing this gripping game, and he has played this game a lot! It's a survival horror game where you play as Daniel, who is exploring a castle full of monsters and traps in 1839, solving puzzles as he goes. It's fun – and scary – to play, especially as Daniel's sanity is reduced as he spends more time in the creepy darkness, making him more vulnerable to hallucinations, and he can pass out, too. There are over 100 videos of Felix playing the game online, including one clip he has titled 'Wet Pants Moment'! The game was followed in 2013 by a sort of sequel, Amnesia: A Machine For Pigs, which PewDiePie also plays on YouTube.

Calling 12

Another horror video game, this one for the WII – this game has a group of characters drawn into a creepy otherworld known as the Mnemonic Abyss via a website known as The Black Page. There are scary schoolgirls, dark corridors, the threat of death and even frightening felines – one of PewDiePie's videos is titled 'Kitty Cat Nearly Killed Me!' thanks to the cat that jumps out in the game, causing Felix to squeal with fright!

Octodad  7

Possibly the weirdest game PewDiePie plays is Octodad
('Loving Father, Caring Husband. Secret Octopus'). Although
he plays a lot of well-known games, Felix likes letting his
YouTube followers know about smaller, independent games
they may not have heard about, and in doing
so he helped make this quirky game popular.
You play as Octodad, who is an octopus
posing as a human man with a family. Yes,
really. You have to complete various tasks to
keep up the charade, while completing your
special mission. And it really is as funny as it
sounds, especially when you watch Felix
playing it.

The Last of Us 18

This is the game that rendered PewDiePie
completely speechless! Fans were used
to hearing him scream, shout and swear
when playing horror games, but when he
videoed himself playing the final part of The
Last of Us, what happened caused him to
go completely silent! We won't reveal it here,
but needless to say it is a jaw-dropper after
you have played the game, the story of Joel
and young Ellie trying to survive after a fungus
has turned people into cannibalistic monsters.
Yuck.

The Walking Dead 18

First there was the comic, then the TV
series, and now the game. Actually,
there are three Walking Dead games

– The Walking Dead, The Walking Dead Season 2, both based on the comics, and The Walking Dead: Survival Instinct, which is more connected to the series. Whichever you choose – and PewDiePie has played them all, of course – you're trying to survive the zombie apocalypse that has turned people into half-dead 'walkers'. Watch out, they're behind you!

Heavy Rain (there are 16 and 18 versions)

Naughty PewDiePie got into trouble when he included a scene from this action game on his YouTube channel in which character Madison took a shower, as even though she's a game character, she was nude! Oops! The game is a thriller that focuses on different people linked with the mystery of the Origami Killer, including journalist Madison, and Ethan, whose son may be the latest victim of the serial murderer.

Journey 7

Another independent game that Felix mentioned on YouTube, Journey, has the player taking on the role of a robed figure in the desert who has to travel through an abandoned city towards a mountain as part of his adventure. PewDiePie has said it's one of the best games he's ever played and recommended it to his Bros after he posted five videos in 2013 of him playing the game online.

And what is the game that PewDiePie thinks is one of the worst of all time? It's Saw II (18), based on the gruesome movies of the same name.

PEWDIEPIE AND CUTIEPIE

It's truly a YouTube romance. Back in 2011, a friend told Italian girl Marzia about an idiot vlogger who screamed while playing games, and suggested she watch him online. Marzia did, and liked what she saw, so she sent PewDiePie a message saying hello and he replied. Soon they were messaging each other and chatting online every day, and when Felix got enough money together he flew to Italy to meet her. 'I did not even tell anyone that I was going away,' he told a Swedish radio station in an interview. 'I just left home and left a note to my parents in the kitchen.' They met for the first time at the arrivals gate of the airport, and have been together ever since – living first in Sweden, then Italy, then briefly in Los Angeles before settling down in Brighton in the summer of 2013.

Both shy at school, Marzia and Felix make a great couple, appearing in each other's videos (Marzia loves horror games too) and raising their two pugs together – when Marzia isn't dressing up in scary costumes to scare the life out of Felix, that is! She also claims she's the one that wears the trousers in their relationship – and since Felix is apparently so forgetful he has missed flights when he's forgotten to go the airport, that is probably a good thing!

Girlfriend Vs Boyfriend

PewDiePie and CutiePieMarzia have done two GF vs BF challenge videos — try some of these challenges yourself with a friend and see if you can beat their scores!

1. The chubby bunny challenge (how many marshmallows you can fit into your mouth): Marzia 7, Felix 15

2. Thumb wrestling: Felix won but Marzia says he cheated!

3. Drawing challenge (draw a picture of the other with your eyes closed): it was, erm, a draw...

4. Cotton-wool ball challenge (scooping as many cotton wool balls into a bowl that's on your head, using a spoon, while blindfolded): Marzia 0, Felix 3

5. Staring contest (see who can stare the longest without blinking): Felix won this one

6. The one-minute make-up challenge — using only food items from your kitchen, see who can make up their face in the best or funniest way! Marzia and Felix used flour, honey, strawberries and we think Marzia won since all Felix managed to do was stick a strawberry up his nose!

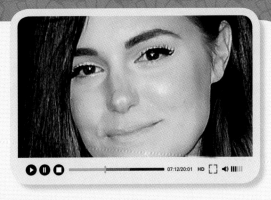

10 Facts about Marzia

1. She is named after her mother's close friend.
2. Marzia can speak Italian, English, French and Spanish.
3. She hates butterflies.
4. She can't burp, even after asking Felix to teach her!
5. Marzia can't be around anyone being sick.
6. Her favourite film is Tim Burton's *Big Fish*.
7. She doesn't like sport at all.
8. Before she met Felix, her plan was to move to Paris and study art.
9. Her favourite book is Oscar Wilde's *The Picture of Dorian Gray*.
10. She has a scar on her chin from when she was pushed over while on roller skates as a kid.

WORDSEARCH

X	B	E	A	Y	S	C	D	W	E	S	G	R	U	M
A	H	O	Y	R	T	I	M	P	U	K	L	S	J	I
Q	D	E	R	E	H	F	L	G	D	P	A	N	O	N
V	R	W	O	G	E	O	X	E	W	U	R	T	M	E
G	Y	P	D	N	L	S	A	M	N	E	S	I	A	C
O	C	T	O	D	A	D	O	W	X	T	N	G	L	R
S	N	A	M	U	S	L	R	P	C	J	H	W	C	A
S	I	L	C	E	T	A	F	D	E	D	T	I	S	F
T	A	G	S	J	O	R	E	S	U	N	R	Y	L	T
H	R	R	D	F	F	P	L	N	W	T	M	W	R	L
A	Y	W	Y	T	U	D	F	O	L	L	A	C	P	W
S	V	O	R	X	S	G	O	U	T	L	A	S	T	O
Z	A	U	C	E	F	A	R	S	P	C	L	E	U	A
W	E	K	P	R	P	N	M	T	C	U	G	S	F	D
T	H	E	W	A	L	K	I	N	G	D	E	A	D	E

PewDiePie is, of course, a huge fan of computer games. Test your knowledge of the games he has talked about and played for his YouTube channel by searching out their names in the word search above. Words can be horizontal, vertical, diagonal and backwards as well as forwards!

OCTODAD

THE LAST OF US

MINECRAFT   HEAVY RAIN

THE WALKING DEAD   GREY

CALL OF DUTY   SILENT HILL

AMNESIA

OUTLAST

Answers on page 64.

INSIDE PEWDIEPIE'S ROOM

PewDiePie grew up in Sweden, spent time living in Italy (his girlfriend Marzia's home) and Los Angeles, and has now settled in Brighton, England, which is quickly becoming the place to live if you are a YouTube vlogger – beauty and fashion queen Zoella, Pointlessblog's Alfie Deyes and Marcus Butler are among those who live in the seaside town. Naturally shy, Felix doesn't want anyone to know exactly where he lives, but we've had a sneaky look, just for you!

Felix lives, of course, with his girlfriend Marzia and their two pug dogs, Edgar and Maya. Their home is a Victorian apartment with high ceilings and pale walls. Their furniture inside is surprisingly old-fashioned – the living room has high-backed chairs, a leather sofa, an antique wood cabinet they bought on eBay, and has paintings in gold frames on the walls, including some of Felix's own artwork.

Of course, the most interesting place is where he films his videos. It's a small room off the kitchen, with a brown leather sofa, a large desk with dual monitor screens, plus lighting, a Blue microphone and other equipment Felix needs to make his clips. The walls feature more of Felix's artwork, including a creepy clown painting, and there's a shelf full of games. Our favourite touches are an R2-D2 toy, a sword ('in case the Nazis ever come back,' PewDiePie said in a video tour of his room), a Cartman from *South Park* figure and Felix's electric guitar.

It's in this room that Felix shouts, screams and yells at the screen while he is playing games – in fact, if you listen when watching the videos Marzia records in their bedroom (you can find her at www.youtube.com/user/CutiePieMarzia), you can often hear Felix shouting at games in the background from his room. No wonder he keeps the windows closed so the neighbours can't hear!

SPOT THE DIFFERENCE

07:12/20:01 HD

60-second challenge!

You have got 60 seconds to spot 5 differences in the photos below.

GO GO GO!

07:12/20:01 HD

Answers on page 64.

PEWDS' PETS

Felix got his chocolate brown pug in October 2013 and named him Edgar after the writer Edgar Allan Poe (the dog's full name is Edgar Allan Pug, of course). He was a year old when Felix brought him home, and to begin with, Edgar wouldn't let Felix and Marzia sleep because he would get lonely!

Edgar is a companion to Maya, their caramel-coloured pug. Marzia posted a video of when the two pugs met, after Maya arrived in Brighton having travelled from their old home in Italy. Maya didn't look massively impressed to have a dog climbing all over her – especially because Edgar is bigger than her – but the two dogs are now best friends.

Marzia has posted the most videos about the two dogs on her channel CutiePieMarzia, including one in April 2014 where she set the two dogs a

competition to see which one was the master pug! Challenges included which dog could run down the stairs fastest (Edgar), a game of hide and seek (Edgar hid under a table, so he won), the blanket escape where they had to free themselves from a blanket (Maya) and a game where they each had to destroy a toy (Edgar). The end result was a draw!

Both dogs live happily with Felix and Marzia in their Brighton home now, and Edgar even has his own YouTube video #EdgarKnows, so he's probably destined to be as big a star as his owners...

TOP 10 PEWDIEPIE MOMENTS

There's a reason Felix has more than 35 million subscribers – he's funny to watch, loves computer games and has a laugh playing them, and he's, well, crazy! Here are 10 of the best PewDiePie moments you can watch on YouTube...

Warning – some contain lots of swearing...

10 Playing Journey for the first time

Felix loves this game in which a caped figure has to make his way across the desert in search of... something. It's really fun watching him play it for the first time as the look of the game is amazing, and as Felix plays he discovers his character can fly, slide down dunes and do barrel rolls when you're exploring. And he even breaks into song while being surrounded by what looks like flying carpets – singing the love theme from *Aladdin*, of course.

www.youtube.com/watch?v=cu9U9LGncPI

9 Scaredy cat

Pewds has had quite a few encounters with cats In his gaming videos, including playing Cat Mario, which he thinks is one of the most frustrating games ever. Best of all, however, is his reaction to a cat running across his character's path in the horror game Calling as he is exploring deserted corridors. Note – this clip has horror elements and swearing! Just skip to 2.45 minutes into the clip to see Felix freak out, and try not to jump yourself!

www.youtube.com/watch?v=j6ckBmW0hpg

8 Grand Theft Auto IV

PewDiePie teamed up with Smosh (Ian Hecox and Anthony Padilla) to play Grand Theft Auto IV and it's one of the silliest things you'll ever see. They get a giraffe and an elephant driving around in one of the cars and are just, well, really silly. Has to be seen to be believed.

https://youtu.be/LBcke5Btoss

7 Happy Wheels Part 1

Pewds has done quite a few Happy Wheels videos but one of the best, and most watched, is the first one he did back in 2012. Playing as characters including Wheelchair Guy, Irresponsible Dad, Lawnmower Man or even Santa Claus, you travel across various obstacles and in this clip the fun is watching Pewds send a poor Grandpa in a wheelchair over some rotating blades ('oh no! you've lost an arm!') and then see Santa be attacked by thunderbolts in a Pokemon gym.

www.youtube.com/watch?v=XW99sBf4BUI

6 A Funny Montage

Felix's first funny montage has had over 60 million views – it's a 10-minute compilation of him playing games (and swearing), shouting and screaming with Marzia online, reading some funny fan fiction, singing (badly), serenading Maya the pug, and leaving the house in Marzia's high heels (and not much else). Stay to the end for a message from Felix.

www.youtube.com/watch?v=gRyPjRrjS34

5 Jabba the Hutt

Schmoyoho wrote a special song for PewDiePie, and in fact it's partly a love song to Maya the pug, otherwise known as Jabba the Hutt. It's filled with clips of the adorable dog, as well as clips of Pewds doing his gaming thing.

www.youtube.com/watch?v=lxw3C5HJ2XU

4 Mean Comments

PewDiePie has millions of fans but he also gets mean comments. In this clip, Felix reads them out and replies to them – including one person who claims Pewds stole his subscribers, one who says he isn't funny, and another who says he is talentless, 'everyone is entitled to their opinion... even though you are *wrong!*'

www.youtube.com/watch?v=5163pfq4xAg

3 Draw My Life

Want to learn more about Felix? This 'draw my life' clip tells the story of his life up to now, including his time at school, meeting Marzia and his love of games. To hear the other side of the story of Marzia and Felix, you can watch her 'Draw My Life' too.

> Felix: www.youtube.com/watch?v=6yBBO8PzWFI
> Marzia: www.youtube.com/watch?v=6yBBO8PzWFI

2 The Impossible Quiz

Fans had suggested Felix play this game in which you answer a series of really silly multiple-choice questions and, in Felix's case, get them wrong again, and again, and again! Sample question: What can you put in a bucket to make it lighter? Possible answers: a) gypsies, b) torch, c) a hole and d) canned laughter (the answer is, of course, b – a torch).

> www.youtube.com/watch?v=rOZ0OHaPmnk

And the best PewDiePie clip ever is:

1 The Last of Us

If you've watched lots of Pewds' videos, you'll be used to him laughing, screaming, swearing and even crying (usually with laughter) as he plays horror and action games. So nothing quite prepares you for the look on his face as he watches the final scenes of the game The Last of Us – stunned into silence, he ends up sitting looking at the screen holding his face in his hands. 'I don't know how I feel about that ending! Why did it have end on a lie?' he says to the screen in puzzlement as he tries to figure it all out. Gulp.

> www.youtube.com/watch?v=wzPJd0aBEM

PEWDS PLAYING DRESS UP

While girlfriend Marzia is the expert at hair, make-up and fashion – and her makeover as the scary Woman in Black was hilarious when she tried to frighten Pewds – it is Felix who has the most fun getting dressed up and made over. Here are some of his best moments:

The Barbie Virtual Makeover

The digital makeover involved Pewds photographing himself and then digitally adding make-up – blue eyeshadow and lips, then pink – with hilarious results. As he says, it's a free app, so go on and 'fabulize yourself'!

How to do a Makeover

Pewds borrowed some of Marzia's make-up and made himself up – complete with beige lips and rather too much eyeliner!

Dressing Up

In his videos, Pewds has also rocked the following outfits:

1. tiara, gold earrings and a pink feather boa
2. a blond wig, bobble hat and make-up
3. black high heels
4. a pink veil with fluffy pom-poms
5. a Sonic the Hedgehog costume
6. an inflatable Sumo wrestler costume
7. a pretty white lace dress

PEWDIEPIE CHALLENGE

Can't think of anything to do today? How about getting together with a friend and testing how well you really know each other? Marzia and Felix have tried the True or False game and now it's your turn.

TRUE

What you need to do:

Grab a good friend.

Each write down 10 things about yourself, some of which are true and some of which are false (but not really obvious ones – you want this to be hard!) and get your friend to do the same. No peeking at the other person's list!

Now take it in turns to ask the other whether a statement is true or false – if someone guesses correctly, they get a point, and the one with the highest score wins.

Finding it tough to think of true/false statements? Here are some examples to get you started...

1. I broke my nose falling off a skateboard
2. I'm scared of... (spiders, thunder, flying, One Direction – you choose)
3. I believe in aliens
4. I'm ambidextrous (can write with both left and right hands)
5. I can do a handstand with one hand

PEWDIEPIE CATCHPHRASES

Fans of Felix don't just watch him to see his game run-throughs, they tune in for his screams (of fear and laughter), his mad sense of humour, and his catchphrases. Here are some of PewDiePie's best-known sayings...

i JUST SCREAM aND EVERYONE laUGHS.

HERE COMES THE BROFIST!

HEY, LET'S WATCH PEWDIEPIE DIE a MILLION TIMES. OH WAIT — THAT'S LIKE EVERY SINGLE 'LET'S PLAY'!

IF PEWDIEPIE WASN'T FAMOUS, HE COULD BE ...

I f Felix hadn't become PewDiePie, he probably would have stayed at university and then had a career in economics. Or maybe stayed behind the scenes being a game designer. But there are some really fun and weird jobs he could have done instead — which one do you think would suit him best? (And yes, these are all real jobs!)

1. Paradise island caretaker

More than 30,000 people applied for this dream job — to live on tropical Hamilton Island off the Great Barrier Reef in Australia for six months and write a blog about it to promote the area to tourists. Ben Southfield was the lucky guy who got to spend his time rent-free in a villa with a pool and get paid over $100,000 for it.

2. Waterslide tester

Yes, there are actually people employed to spend their days flying down waterslides or trying not to throw up on rollercoasters. These employees are checking slides for speed, water quantity and safety, and rollercoasters for safety, speed and excitement. Scream if you want to go faster!

3. Funeral clown

It's traditional for attendees at a circus performer's funeral to dress up in their circus costumes or come as clowns, but non-circus folk can have a clown at their funeral now, too. You can hire clowns to appear at your funeral or wake, and they'll make balloon animals to bring a smile to the faces of mourners.

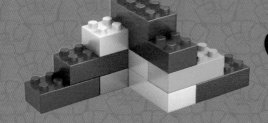

4. LEGO sculptor

Get paid to play like a kid! The famous plastic brick making company employs people to create and build models before they become the kits you can buy in the shops. There are also LEGO staff members whose job it is to make those amazing sculptures that you see in LEGOLANDs around the world in Denmark, California, Germany, Florida, Malaysia and England, from models of famous buildings to the giant dragon in the water outside the LEGO store in Downtown Disney in Orlando.

5. Professional sleeper

Want to be paid to take a nap? Some lucky people, usually for university studies on sleep or dreams, get to do just that, while people have also been paid to sleep on beds in hotels to test their softness, and sleep for art – at the New Museum of Contemporary Art women slept as part of a living art exhibition. Zzzzzz.

6. Ferrari driving instructor

Teaching people to drive must usually be quite boring if you're in some slow family car, but not if you get to do it in a sports car. Former racing drivers teach people how to drive 150mph cars like Ferraris, and also get to sit in the passenger seat on race track days at places like Silverstone and Brands Hatch in England, where anyone over 21 with a valid driving licence can pay to do a few laps around the track in a powerful sports car.

7. Nail polish namer

Look at the base of a bottle of nail polish and you'll see the colour isn't simply called 'red' or 'pink' or 'black' – oh no, it's 'Scallywag' (actually a blue glittery one), 'Shattered Souls' (gold glitter), 'It's Raining Men' (a red) or 'Bikini So Teeny' (pale blue). And yes, someone really does get paid to come up with these names...

TOMATO KETCHUP X

ZOMBIE ENTRAILS X

NOSE BLEED X

8. Monkey chaser

Some of the most luxurious resorts in India employ people simply to scare away monkeys! The cute little creatures have a habit of scampering about, stealing any food left lying about and occasionally pooping where they shouldn't to the annoyance of guests, so there are attendants whose job it is to shoo the primates away.

9. Shark tank cleaner

Not one for the faint hearted, this job requires you to get into scuba gear, jump into a shark tank at an aquarium, and clean the windows while sharks are swimming about, just so that people who come to the exhibit can see in (and so the sharks can see out, presumably). While the sharks will probably leave you alone, you just know some of the onlookers are secretly hoping you'll get eaten...

10. Oshiya (passenger pusher)

Japan's trains are renowned for being incredibly crowded during rush hour, and to help with the problem there are people whose job it is to push people onto the trains, shoving as many people as possible into each train carriage. They were originally called 'passenger arrangement staff', which sounds more impressive.

THE ULTIMATE PEWD

Think you know everything about Felix and his life? Then take the quiz below to find out how much you really know about the world's most successful YouTuber...

Answers on page 64.

1. Which fan club did Felix join as a child in Sweden, becoming the youngest ever member?

a) The Sherlock Holmes club
b) The Doctor Who club
c) The Star Wars club
d) The James Bond club

2. Felix has an older sister – but what is her name?

a) Frida
b) Fifi
c) Fanny
d) Frances

3. One of Felix's dogs is a little different from the other – do you know how?

a) Edgar has a brown nose and Maya has a black one
b) Maya has a white spot of fur and Edgar doesn't
c) Edgar is deaf
d) Maya only has one eye

4. Felix is, of course, Swedish, and sometimes starts speaking his native language in his videos. He posted a video explaining useful Swedish sentences, so tell us – what does 'bra' mean in Swedish?

a) good
b) bad
c) underwear
d) hat

5) In June 2014, how much money did PewDiePie help raise for Save The Children to celebrate reaching 25 million YouTube subscribers?

a) $250,000
b) $100,000
c) $630,000
d) $480,000

6) In 2014, Felix and Marzia made some videos as part of a marketing campaign for a new scary movie. What movie was it?

a) *Dracula Untold*
b) *As Above, So Below*
c) *The Babadook*
d) *Horns*

7) If he wasn't a vlogger, what has PewDiePie said he'd want to do for a living?

a) a rock guitarist
b) a games designer/creator
c) a horror movie director
d) a radio DJ

EPIE QUIZ

8) Felix has appeared as himself in a cartoon series. Which one?

a) *South Park*
b) *The Simpsons*
c) *Family Guy*
d) *Adventure Time*

9) How many NEW subscribers do you think PewDiePie earned in 2014?

a) 14 million
b) 20 million
c) 5 million
d) 10 million

10) Months before they met, Marzia's friend sent her a PewDiePie video. What did the friend describe him as?

a) a brilliant gamer
b) an idiot
c) a joker
d) handsome

11) Which of these creatures does PewDiePie say he believes in?

a) aliens
b) ghosts
c) vampires
d) zombies

12) A song called 'His Name is PewDiePie' was recorded in 2014. Who made it?

a) Buddy
b) Roomie
c) PewDiePie
d) Marzia

13) Why did Marzia and Felix move to England?

a) their internet connection in Italy was terrible
b) Felix's family had moved there
c) Marzia was offered a job there
d) Felix found the weather in Italy was too hot for him

14) Which of these is **NOT** a real game that PewDiePie has played?

a) Goat Simulator
b) Octodad
c) Conkers' Bad Fur Day
d) Bonkers Duck

15) One of PewDiePie's closest YouTube friends is CinnamonToastKen. What's his real name?

a) Kenneth Branagh
b) Kenneth Williams
c) Kenneth Morrison
d) Kenneth Sainsbury

THE FUTURE

So what's next for PewDiePie? As the owner of the most subscribed channel on YouTube, he's already the most popular YouTuber on the planet! He has said that working on his videos takes up so much time that he may retire from doing it altogether in a few years, but in the meantime he has an empire to run – as well as his videos, TV appearances and time spent raising money for charity, Pewds has also launched his own shop, featuring clothes and accessories with his Brofist logo on them.

Whatever he chooses to do, it's sure to be a success. Perhaps he'll write a book about pug dogs or create a graphic novel, make his own video game, design some really cool headphones for game playing, or travel the world with Marzia. Felix is only in his twenties, and already a millionaire with more than a billion views on YouTube, so the sky really is the limit for... PewDiePie!

STAY AWESOME, BROS.

07:12/20:01 HD

ANSWER PAGE

```
X B E A Y S C D W E S G R U M
A H O Y R T I M P U K L S J I
Q D E R E H F L G D P A N O N
V R W O G E O X E W U R T M E
G Y P D N L S A M N E S I A C
O C T O D A D O W X T N G L R
S N A M U S L R P C J H W C A
S I L C E T A F D E D T I S F
T A G S J O R E S U N R Y L T
H R R D F F P L N W T M W R L
A Y W Y T U D F O L L A C P W
S V O R X S G O U T L A S T O
Z A U C E F A R S P C L E U A
W E K P R P N M T C U G S F D
T H E W A L K I N G D E A D E
```

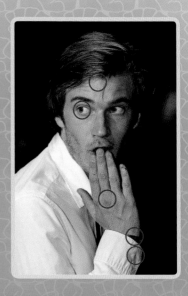

TRUE OR FALSE

1) False — they met online. 2) True.
3) True. 4) False — he hasn't lived
in Spain but he did live in Italy for a
time. 5) False — she posts fashion and
beauty videos. 6) True. 7) True. 8) False
— their names are Maya and Edgar.
9) False — sort of. Felix was asked to
be in a movie playing himself but it
was never actually made. 10) True.
11) False — he only records them a day
or two ahead, after reading comments
from fans. 12) False. 13) True. 14) True.
15) True.

THE ULTIMATE PEWDIEPIE QUIZ

1) a; 2) c; 3) d; 4) a; 5) c; 6) b; 7) b;
8) a; 9) a; 10) b; 11) a; 12) b; 13) a;
14) d; 15) c.

With special thanks to
Danny Fawcett.